THE ULTIMATE
ASTON VILLA FC
TRIVIA BOOK

A Collection of Amazing Trivia Quizzes
and Fun Facts for Die-Hard Lions Fans!

Ray Walker

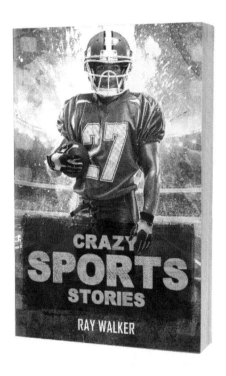

CONTENTS

INTRODUCTION

Aston Villa has been delivering exhilarating performances on the soccer scene in the UK and Europe ever since being formed way back in 1874. They've faced some stiff local competition over the years from the likes of Birmingham City, West Bromwich Albion, and Wolverhampton Wanderers, but Villa is still going strong and pulling in the crowds.

The club's fans, often affectionately known as "Villans," are loyal, passionate, and as vocal as any in the world when they get behind their team.

Villa tasted success early by winning several league and FA Cup titles before World War II and then endured several lean years. In fact, the side was even relegated to the Third Division at one point.

However, the club bounced back as usual and reclaimed its rightful place in the top tier of English soccer. Not only that, but Villa also became just the third English and fourth British outfit to hit the jackpot and be crowned champions of Europe on that glorious night in 1982.

The silverware may have dried up over the past several years, but the team is still as entertaining and dramatic as it's always been. The club's loyal fans will always be there through thick and thin, and with support like that, it shouldn't be long until the Villa squad again hoists a trophy at Villa Park or Wembley.

This Aston Villa book you're holding in your hands features a multitude of trivia, facts, and information about the club from its roots in the nineteenth century up until the conclusion of the 2021 January transfer window.

It includes educational facts and figures about all the greatest Villa players and managers in history, including Charlie Aitken, Billy Walker, Gordon Cowans, Nigel Spink, Gareth Barry, Dennis Mortimer, Eric Houghton, George Ramsay, Jimmy Rimmer, Gareth Southgate, Brian Little, Dwight Yorke, Peter Withe, David Platt, Gabriel Agbonlahor, and Jack Grealish.

You'll be presented with 12 chapters of Villa trivia, with each featuring a unique topic. Each chapter contains 20 multiple-choice and true-false questions, with answers on a separate page. The chapters are also highlighted with 10 "Did You Know" facts and anecdotes about the club.

This is the ideal way to freshen up on your Aston Villa history and test it by challenging fellow fans, friends, and family members in Villa trivia contests. The book is meant to educate and entertain while bringing back memorable moments to the team's supporters.

Villa may not be the consistent trophy-winning team of the past, but the club's fans are still right behind them each and every time they take to the pitch.

Hopefully, this fascinating trivia book will remind you why you've always been such a passionate Villa supporter and will continue to be so.

CHAPTER 1:

ORIGINS & HISTORY

QUIZ TIME!

1. In what year was Aston Villa founded?

    a. 1888

    b. 1882

    c. 1874

    d. 1866

2. Aston Villa has been relegated twice in the Premier League era as of 2020.

    a. True

    b. False

3. From 1874 to 1876, the team played most of its home games where?

    a. Aston Park

    b. Heathfield Road

    c. Villa Park

    d. Wellington Road

4. What motto did Villa feature on its crest from 1992 to 2016?

    a. Courage

    b. Dedicated

    c. Honor

    d. Prepared

5. What are the official kit colors of Aston Villa?

    a. Claret and blue

    b. Burgundy and sky blue

    c. Red and white

    d. Maroon and navy

6. Who did Villa play their first match against?

    a. West Bromwich Albion

    b. Aston Brook St. Mary's Rugby Team

    c. Birmingham City FC

    d. Preston North End

7. Aston Villa was one of the original 22 teams to join the Premier League in 1992-93.

    a. True

    b. False

8. What was the outcome of Villa's first official match in 1874?

    a. 4-1 win

    b. 7-7 draw

    c. win

    d. 12-3 loss

9. How many variations of Villa's crest have been used in the club's history?

    a. 5

    b. 6

    c. 8

    d. 11

10. Who was NOT one of the four key founders of Aston Villa?

    a. Walter Price

    b. Frederick Matthews

    c. Jack Hughes

    d. William McGregor

11. How many times has Villa been relegated in their history as of 2020?

    a. 1

    b. 3

    c. 6

    d. 9

12. Villa played half of its first official match in 1874 with rugby rules and the other half with association football rules.

    a. True

    b. False

13. What was the first major league Villa played in?

    a. Midlands Pro League

    b. English Football League

c. The Combination

d. Football Alliance

14. In 2007, Villa added a white star to the crest to signify a victory in what major competition?

    a. UEFA Cup

    b. Birmingham Senior Cup

    c. European Cup

    d. FA Cup

15. Which is NOT one of Aston Villa's nicknames?

    a. The Lions

    b. The Claret and Blue Army

    c. The Villa

    d. Aston's Finest

16. Aston Villa played its first official league match in 1891.

    a. True

    b. False

17. Aston Villa's inaugural match at Villa Park was a 3-0 win over which club?

    a. Stafford Road

    b. Nottingham Forrest FC

    c. Blackburn Rovers

    d. Huddersfield Town

18. Against which club did Villa play its first official league match?

    a. Wolverhampton Wanderers

    b. Notts County FC

c. Accrington FC

d. West Bromwich Albion

19. What was the final score of Villa's first official league match?

    a. win

    b. draw

    c. 0-2 loss

    d. 2-4 loss

20. Aston Villa secretary Frederick Rinder was one of the founders of the English Football League.

    a. True

    b. False

QUIZ ANSWERS

1. C – 1874

2. B – False

3. A – Aston Park

4. D – Prepared

5. A – Claret and blue

6. B – Aston Brook St. Mary's Rugby Team

7. A – True

8. C – 1-0 win

9. C – 8

10. D – William McGregor

11. C – 6

12. A – True

13. B – English Football League

14. C – European Cup

15. D – Aston's Finest

16. B – False

17. C – Blackburn Rovers

18. A – Wolverhampton Wanderers

19. B – 1-1 draw

20. B – False

DID YOU KNOW?

1. The Aston Villa Football Club, which played in the English Premier League in the 2020-21 season, was founded in March 1874. The team is based in the Aston section of the city of Birmingham, England. Its nicknames are the Villa, the Lions, and the Claret and Blue Army. The club is also known typically just as Villa or AVFC, and its supporters are often known as "Villans."

2. The team has played its home games at Villa Park stadium since 1897. As of February 2021, the venue had a capacity of 42,749 fans. The club is currently owned by Egyptian businessman Nassef Sawiris and American businessman Wesley Edens, with Sawiris as the acting club chairman. The company that owns Villa is the NSWE Group, which represents the initials of the two men.

3. The club was originally formed by several members of the Villa Cross Wesleyan Chapel, which was located in the Handsworth section of Birmingham. The four major founders were Frederick Matthews, Jack Hughes, William Scattergood, and Walter Price.

4. The team's first known match was against a local rugby team known as Aston Brook St. Mary's in March 1874, with Villa winning 1-0. The first half of the contest was played under rugby rules, while the second stanza was played under Football Association rules.

5. From 1874 to 1876, the team played most of its home matches at Aston Park and then moved to Wellington Road, while quickly establishing itself as one of the best squads in the Midlands area. The first piece of silverware hoisted by the outfit was the 1880 Birmingham Senior Cup. George Ramsay of Scotland was then the acting captain.

6. In 1887, Villa captured the English FA Cup for the first time under captain Archie Hunter, and a year later, the side competed in the inaugural English Football League with 11 other teams. One of the founders of the league was an Aston Villa director, William McGregor.

7. The club moved to the Aston Lower Grounds in 1897, and fans quickly began referring to the venue as "Villa Park." In the Victorian era, Aston Villa was regarded as the most successful English club, as it won three FA Cups and five First Division league titles by 1901, which was the end of Queen Victoria's reign. The squad also managed to pull off the league and FA Cup double in 1897.

8. By 1920, Aston Villa had won six FA Cup titles. However, the team began to decline and was relegated to the Second Division for the first time in 1935-36 after conceding 110 goals in their 42 league outings that season.

9. The English Football Association competitions were placed on hold for seven years due to World War II and that spelled the end to numerous playing careers. The club was then rebuilt under manager Alex Massie following the

worldwide conflict. It finally ended a 36-year drought by winning its first trophy in 1956-57, when it captured a then-record seventh FA Cup, downing the famous Manchester United "Busby Babes" side.

10. Aston Villa was relegated again two years after winning its record-setting FA Cup but bounced back to the top flight a year later by winning the Second Division. The club then made history again by becoming the first side to win the inaugural English Football League Cup in 1960-61.

CHAPTER 2:

THE CAPTAIN CLASS

QUIZ TIME!

1. Who was the club's first known official captain?

   a. Jack Devey

   b. Archie Hunter

   c. George Ramsay

   d. Walter H. Price

2. Villa has had 50 different full-time captains as of 2020.

   a. True

   b. False

3. Who succeeded Tommy Elphick as captain in 2016-17?

   a. Micah Richards

   b. James Chester

   c. Alan Hutton

   d. Jed Steer

4. Who succeeded Kevin Richardson as captain in 1995-96?

   a. Nigel Spink

   b. Gareth Southgate

c. Andy Townsend

d. Stuart Gray

5. How many different players acted as full-time captains between 2010 and 2020?

    a. 8

    b. 6

    c. 5

    d. 3

6. Who followed Ron Vlaar as skipper in 2015?

    a. Ciaran Clark

    b. Gabriel Agbonlahor

    c. Fabian Delph

    d. Micah Richards

7. Aston Villa named three different captains in the 1966-67 season.

    a. True

    b. False

8. Which of the following players was never named full-time captain of Aston Villa?

    a. Gordon Cowans

    b. Dennis Mortimer

    c. Allan Evans

    d. Vic Crowe

9. Who was Villa's first captain born outside of the British Isles?

a. Martin Laursen

b. Olof Mellberg

c. Stiliyan Petrov

d. Ron Vlaar

10. Chris Nicholl succeeded which player as captain?

a. Jack Devey

b. Alan Deakin

c. Charlie Aitken

d. Ian Ross

11. Which skipper was born in Bulgaria?

a. Gabriel Agbonlahor

b. Jack Grealish

c. Alex Massie

d. Stiliyan Petrov

12. Charlie Aitken was Villa's shortest-serving full-time captain as of 2020.

a. True

b. False

13. Which player followed Gareth Southgate as captain in 2001-02?

a. Jlloyd Samuel

b. Steve Stone

c. Paul Merson

d. Ian Taylor

14. Skipper Gareth Southgate left Villa for which club in 2009?

a. Peterborough United

b. West Bromwich Albion

c. Manchester City

d. Liverpool

15. Who was the Villa captain in 2003 immediately before Olof Mellberg?

a. Steve Staunton

b. Peter Crouch

c. Ian Taylor

d. Alan Wright

16. Chris Nicholl was Villa's final captain before the club joined the Premier League.

a. True

b. False

17. Which player did Villa appoint as captain in 2019-20?

a. Jack Grealish

b. Douglas Luiz

c. Tyrone Mings

d. John McGinn

18. Which former Villa skipper holds the record for most Premier League games played in history?

a. Chris Sutton

b. Steven Davis

c. Gareth Barry

d. Ashley Young

19. How many Villa captains were born in Denmark?

    a. 0

    b. 1

    c. 3

    d. 5

20. Kevin Richardson was the squad's first captain in the Premier League era.

    a. True

    b. False

QUIZ ANSWERS

1. D – Walter H. Price
2. B – False
3. B – James Chester
4. C – Andy Townsend
5. A – 8
6. C – Fabian Delph
7. B – False
8. A – Gordon Cowans
9. B – Olof Mellberg
10. D – Ian Ross
11. D – Stiliyan Petrov
12. B – False
13. C – Paul Merson
14. C – Manchester City
15. A – Steve Staunton
16. B – False
17. A – Jack Grealish
18. C – Gareth Barry
19. B – 1
20. A – True

DID YOU KNOW?

1. Because Aston Villa was formed way back in 1874, it's close to impossible to put together a complete list of full-time captains for the club. However, it's believed the team has had approximately 42 full-time captains throughout its history, with the first being Walter H. Price, one of the club's founding members, and the most recent being Jack Grealish, who was appointed in 2019.

2. The 42 known full-time skippers have represented nine different nationalities. Twenty-five of the captains have been English, while seven were Scottish, three were Welsh, two were from the Republic of Ireland, and one was Northern Irish. One each represented the nations of Holland, Denmark, Bulgaria, and Sweden.

3. The first non-British or -Irish full-time captain was Swedish defender Olof Mellberg, who also skippered his national side. He joined the squad in 2001 from Racing Santander in Spain and remained until 2008 when he left for Juventus of Italy. Mellberg resigned as captain following the 2006 World Cup and handed the armband to Gareth Barry. Mellberg's last game for Villa was in May 2008 away to West Ham United. He gave each Villa fan at the game one of his shirts with the message "Thanks 4 Your Support" on it.

4. Center-back Martin Laursen was a Danish international who finished his career with Villa, from 2004 to 2009, after

joining from AC Milan. He was voted the Supporters' Player of the Year for 2007-08 and was named Danish Player of the Year for 2008. Unfortunately, he retired in 2009 due to a knee injury after scoring 11 goals in 91 matches with the club. Laursen then became a football manager and TV pundit.

5. Bulgaria's most-capped player was midfielder Stiliyan Petrov, with 105 games to his name. He was Villa skipper for several years while playing for the side from 2006 to 2012. Petrov appeared in over 200 games before being diagnosed with acute leukemia in March 2012. He successfully underwent treatment but hung up his boots in May 2013. Three years later, he trained with Villa and played several pre-season contests but wasn't offered a contract. Petrov was the club's Players' Player of the Year for 2008-09 and 2011-12 and the Supporters' Player of the Year for 2008-09. He was also inducted into the Aston Villa Hall of Fame.

6. Dutch international defender Ron Vlaar was skipper of Feyenoord in his homeland before joining Villa in 2012. He then wore the armband with his new club to replace the ill Stiliyan Petrov before returning to Holland in 2015 to play for AZ Alkmaar, where he had begun his pro career. Vlaar suffered several injuries with Villa but still managed to play nearly 90 games. He helped the side reach the 2014-15 FA Cup final, where they were beaten 4-0 by Arsenal.

7. The first captain to win an FA Cup was forward Archie Hunter in 1887. The Scotsman played with the team from

1878 to 1890 and reportedly netted 43 goals in 74 games, with his 33 FA Cup markers being a team record. He also scored in every round of the 1887 FA Cup tournament. Hunter was one of the best players of his era but never played for Scotland because Scotsmen who played in the English League couldn't represent their homeland at that time. In 1890, Hunter suffered a heart attack in a game against Everton and never played again. He passed away four years later at the age of 35. His brother Andy also played for Villa and scored their first-ever FA Cup goal.

8. English international striker John "Jack" Devey represented Villa between 1891 and 1902, and his 20 goals in 1893-94 helped them in the league. His 183 goals in 311 games ranks third all-time on the club scoring list. Devey captained the side for eight years and led his teammates to five league titles and two FA Cups between 1894 and 1900. This included the league and cup double in 1896-97. Devey retired in 1902 and became an Aston Villa director for 32 years. He was also a first-class cricket player and played pro baseball for Aston Villa in the National League of Baseball of Great Britain in 1890.

9. Former England and Chelsea captain John Terry capped off his legendary career with Villa in the second-tier English Football League Championship in 2017-18 and was captain for the season. Terry had won numerous team and individual trophies with Chelsea and led Villa to the Championship League playoff final, where they were edged 1-0 by Fulham. Terry remained with the club as a

member of new manager Dean Smith's management team. The squad won the 2018-19 Championship playoff final 2-1 against Derby County and was promoted back to the Premier League.

10. Tommy Elphick joined Villa from Bournemouth in 2016 and remained until 2019 before leaving for Huddersfield Town. However, the native of England was sent on loan to Reading and Hull City in 2018 before being released. He was Villa's first signing after the club was relegated to the second-tier Championship League in 2015-16 and was named skipper before the 2016-17 campaign kicked off. He was replaced as full-time captain during the season by James Chester, though, because Elphick often found himself on the substitutes' bench.

CHAPTER 3:

AMAZING MANAGERS

QUIZ TIME!

1. How many men held the full-time manager's position between 2010 and 2020?

    a. 5

    b. 7

    c. 9

    d. 10

2. Until 1934, the Villa team was selected by the players only.

    a. True

    b. False

3. Whom did Ron Saunders succeed as manager in 1974?

    a. Tommy Docherty

    b. Vic Crowe

    c. Tony Barton

    d. Tommy Cummings

4. Which club did Roberto Di Matteo manage before being hired by Aston Villa?

   a. FC Zürich
   b. West Bromwich Albion
   c. Chelsea FC
   d. FC Schalke 04

5. Who was Villa's first known full-time official manager?

   a. Jimmy McMullan
   b. W.J. Smith
   c. Gordon Ramsay
   d. Jimmy Hogan

6. Which club did Ron Saunders manage after leaving Aston Villa?

   a. Norwich City
   b. Oxford United
   c. Birmingham City FC
   d. Manchester City

7. Jozef Vengloš is recognized as the first manager born outside of the British Isles to be hired by a top-tier team in Britain.

   a. True
   b. False

8. Whom did Dean Smith follow as manager in 2018?

   a. Tim Sherwood
   b. Rémi Garde
   c. Roberto Di Matteo
   d. Steve Bruce

9. Which club did Paul Lambert manage before joining Villa?

   a. Stoke City
   b. Colchester United
   c. Wolverhampton Wanderers
   d. Norwich City

10. Who replaced Brian Little as boss in 1998?

   a. George Martin
   b. David O'Leary
   c. John Gregory
   d. Graham Taylor

11. Who succeeded Jozef Vengloš as manager in 1991?

   a. Alex Massie
   b. Ron Atkinson
   c. Brian Little
   d. Graham Taylor

12. Roberto Di Matteo managed Villa for just 12 matches before being fired.

   a. True
   b. False

13. Which manager did Paul Lambert succeed in 2012?

   a. Martin O'Neill
   b. Alex McLeish
   c. Gérard Houllier
   d. David O'Leary

14. Which club did Jozef Vengloš manage after leaving Aston Villa?

    a. Celtic FC

    b. Fenerbahçe S.K.

    c. Sporting CP

    d. Kuala Lumpur FA

15. Who won three trophies while managing Villa?

    a. Joe Mercer

    b. Tony Barton

    c. Brian Little

    d. Ron Saunders

16. George Ramsay was the club's longest-serving secretary/manager, holding the position for 42 years.

    a. True

    b. False

17. How many stints did Graham Taylor serve as Villa manager?

    a. 2

    b. 4

    c. 3

    d. 5

18. Which manager won the 1995-96 League Cup?

    a. Ron Atkinson

    b. John Gregory

    c. Brian Little

    d. Graham Taylor

19. Which club did Steve Bruce manage before being hired by Villa?

    a. Atlético Madrid
    b. Sheffield Wednesday
    c. Manchester United
    d. Kettering Town FC

20. Tony Barton managed Villa to the 1981-82 European Cup title.

    a. True
    b. False

QUIZ ANSWERS

1. C – 9

2. B – False

3. B – Vic Crowe

4. D – FC Schalke 04

5. A – Jimmy McMullan

6. C – Birmingham City FC

7. A – True

8. D – Steve Bruce

9. D – Norwich City

10. C – John Gregory

11. B – Ron Atkinson

12. A – True

13. B – Alex McLeish

14. B – Fenerbahçe S.K.

15. D – Ron Saunders

16. A – True

17. A – 2

18. C – Brian Little

19. B – Sheffield Wednesday

20. A – True

DID YOU KNOW?

1. Between 1874 and 1934, the Aston Villa team was chosen by a committee whose secretary held the same role and powers as a modern-day manager. During this period, there were two secretaries, George Ramsay and W. J. Smith. Jimmy McMullan, who was appointed in 1934, was believed to be the club's first full-time manager.

2. The turnover rate of Villa managers has substantially increased during the past 30 years. Former club chairman Doug Ellis was nicknamed "Deadly Doug" due to his habit of hiring and firing managers. Ellis was on the Aston Villa board for 37 years and was responsible for hiring and firing 13 of the side's full-time managers.

3. Aston Villa was recognized as being the first top-tier club in England to hire a manager who hailed from outside of the United Kingdom and Ireland. This took place in July 1990 when Jozef Vengloš of the former nation of Czechoslovakia was named the new boss. However, he was gone less than a year later when Ron Atkinson replaced him in 1991.

4. Ron Atkinson was in charge between July 1991 and November 1994 and guided the side to the runner-up position in the very first Premier League season in 1992-93. He also won the 1993-94 League Cup. Atkinson was signed by Villa as a player at the age of 17 but never made

a first-team appearance. He set a club record for games played with Oxford United at over 500 and played alongside his brother Graham. Atkinson also managed Manchester United, Atlético Madrid, and several other clubs during his career.

5. The most successful manager/secretary in Villa history was George Ramsay, who held the position from 1884 to 1926. His 42 years in charge makes him the longest-serving boss in the club's annals. Ramsay helped his team capture six FA Cup and First Division titles for a total of 12 trophies. He had previously played with the squad as one of its first captains. The native of Scotland hung up his boots in 1892, and, after managing the side, he became a club vice-president.

6. When George Ramsay left his post as club manager/secretary in 1926, he was replaced by W.J. "Billy" Smith of England. Smith held the post until 1934 when he stepped down after guiding the team to two runner-up finishes in the First Division. He had joined the club in 1910 when he was just 17 years old and remained with Aston Villa until passing away 47 years later.

7. The first full-time modern-day position of manager was held by Jimmy McMullan, who had played in his homeland of Scotland and also with Manchester City before retiring as a player. He helped manage Maidstone United and Oldham Athletic before taking the reins at Villa from 1934 to 1936. Things didn't go well for McMullan with Villa,

though, as the team was relegated from the First to Second Division in 1935-36 following a run of 61 years in the top flight.

8. The last manager to hoist any domestic silverware with Villa was Englishman Brian Little, who guided the side to the 1995-96 League Cup. The last manager to win anything in Europe was John Gregory of England, who led the squad to the 2001 Intertoto Cup. In 2018-19, current manager Dean Smith, who was appointed in October 2018, led the players to a 2-1 decision over Derby County in the second-tier Football League Championship to earn promotion back to the Premier League.

9. Eric Houghton is currently the only Villa manager to win the FA Cup since World War II. He guided the team to the title in 1956-57 with a 2-1 win over Manchester United. Joe Mercer led the team to its first league cup in 1960-61 as well as winning the Second Division title the previous season. The only other manager to win the Second Division with the team was Jimmy Hogan in 1937-38, and the only man in charge to capture the Third Division was Vic Crowe in 1971-72.

10. Former Celtic, Arsenal, and Chelsea player Tommy Docherty of Scotland entered the world of football management in 1961 as a player-manager with Chelsea. He took over the full-time job soon afterward and remained in London until 1967. Docherty was named Villa manager in December 1968 but was fired 13 months later

by chairman Doug Ellis. When he was sacked, the team was buried in last place in the Second Division, and Docherty had won just 13 of 46 games. Docherty would go on to manage another 11 teams including Scotland, Porto, and Manchester United.

CHAPTER 4:

GOALTENDING GREATS

QUIZ TIME!

1. Which keeper recorded 46 Premier League clean sheets for the team?

    a. Shay Given

    b. David James

    c. Thomas Sørensen

    d. Brad Friedel

2. Nigel Spink made his debut for Villa in the 1982 European Cup final.

    a. True

    b. False

3. Who backed up Tom Heaton in 12 Premier League games in 2019-20?

    a. Sam Johnstone

    b. Jed Steer

    c. Pepe Reina

    d. Örjan Nyland

4. How many appearances did Peter Schmeichel make for Villa in all competitions?

    a. 44
    b. 36
    c. 29
    d. 23

5. Who backed up Nigel Spink in 17 matches in the inaugural Premier League season of 1992-93?

    a. Mark Bosnich
    b. Les Sealy
    c. Michael Oakes
    d. Kevin Poole

6. Which keeper made 29 appearances during the 1999-2000 Premier League campaign?

    a. David James
    b. Michael Oakes
    c. Neil Cutler
    d. Adam Rachel

7. Peter Schmeichel recorded 10 clean sheets in all competitions for Villa.

    a. True
    b. False

8. Which keeper has made the most appearances for Villa in all competitions as of 2020?

    a. Nigel Sims
    b. Jimmy Rimmer

c. Nigel Spink

d. Billy George

9. In how many English Championship Division contests did Pierluigi Gollini play in 2016-17?

    a. 13

    b. 17

    c. 20

    d. 25

10. Which keeper played all 38 matches in the 2009-10 Premier League season?

    a. Brad Guzan

    b. Brad Friedel

    c. Stuart Taylor

    d. Shay Given

11. How many clean sheets did Mark Bosnich record in the 1995-96 Premier League campaign?

    a. 2

    b. 9

    c. 12

    d. 15

12. Peter Schmeichel once scored a goal for Villa in a Premier League match against Everton FC.

    a. True

    b. False

13. Who recorded 22 clean sheets in the 2017-18 English Championship Division?

a. Sam Johnstone

b. Mark Bunn

c. Jed Steer

d. Pierluigi Gollini

14. Which keeper played 35 matches in the 2007-08 Premier League season?

a. Brad Guzan

b. Gábor Király

c. Scott Carson

d. Geoff Sidebottom

15. How many clean sheets did Tom Heaton record in the 2019-20 Premier League season?

a. 13

b. 9

c. 4

d. 2

16. Nigel Spink made over 500 appearances for Villa in all competitions.

a. True

b. False

17. In how many English Championship Division matches did Sam Johnstone play in 2017-18?

a. 15

b. 23

c. 36

d. 45

18. Which keeper was signed from Manchester United and returned there in 1999?

    a. Thomas Sørensen
    b. Mark Bosnich
    c. David James
    d. Stefan Postma

19. How many clean sheets did Pepe Reina record in the 2019-20 Premier League?

    a. 9
    b. 5
    c. 2
    d. 0

20. Brad Guzan played all 38 matches in the 2013-14 Premier League season.

    a. True
    b. False

QUIZ ANSWERS

1. C – Thomas Sørensen

2. B – False

3. C – Pepe Reina

4. B – 36

5. A – Mark Bosnich

6. A – David James

7. B – False

8. C – Nigel Spink

9. C – 20

10. B – Brad Friedel

11. D – 15

12. A – True

13. A – Sam Johnstone

14. C – Scott Carson

15. C – 4

16. B – False

17. D – 45

18. B – Mark Bosnich

19. C – 2

20. A – True

DID YOU KNOW?

1. Nigel Spink is a Villa legend after playing over 450 games with the club between 1977 and 1996 to set a team record for most games by a goalkeeper. Spink, who had played just one first-team game up to then, had to fill in for starting keeper Jimmy Rimmer in the 1982 European Cup final when Rimmer left the match with an injury in the first 10 minutes. Spink played the game of his life and shut out Bayern Munich to win the championship. He then helped the side capture the 1982 European Super Cup and the 1993-94 League Cup. Spink left Villa in 1996 for West Bromwich Albion.

2. Australian international Mark "Bozzie" Bosnich played between the posts from 1992 to 1999 after signing on a free transfer from Manchester United. He helped the team haul in the league cup in 1993-94 and 1995-96. Bosnich made a trio of sensational saves in the semifinal penalty shootout against Tranmere Rovers in 1994 as Villa came from behind and advanced to the final. He appeared in over 200 games with the club before heading back to Manchester United on a free transfer.

3. After joining from Wolverhampton in 1956, Nigel Sims proved he had a pair of safe hands and plenty of agility as he helped Villa beat Manchester United in the FA Cup final the next season. He then helped the side capture the

1959-60 Second Division title and promotion back to the top flight. Sims wasn't finished: He also won the league cup with the team in 1960-61. He was the first winner of Aston Villa supporters' Terrace Trophy in 1958 and left for Peterborough United in 1964 before playing in Canada.

4. After being named Player of the Year for Arsenal in 1975, Jimmy Rimmer joined Villa in 1977 for £65,000. He took over the number-one job from John Burridge and played over 270 games in the next six years before leaving for Swansea City in 1983. Rimmer helped Villa win the 1980-81 First Division title as well as the 1981-82 European Cup and 1982 European Super Cup. Rimmer had helped Manchester United win the 1967-68 European Cup and became just the second player to win the trophy with two different teams.

5. Known as "The Human Wall," American international Brad Friedel joined Villa from Blackburn Rovers in 2008 for £2.5 million and remained until 2011 when he joined Tottenham Hotspur. Friedel broke the record for consecutive Premier League games in November 2008 at 167. He was sent off with a red card against Liverpool later in the season. However, the FA overturned the decision; Friedel continued his streak and reached 250 straight league games in January 2011. He also became the oldest player to ever play for Villa in February 2011 at the age of 40 years and four days.

6. Villa had two American international keepers at the same time, as Brad Guzan played from 2008 to 2016 while being

loaned to Hull City for a spell in 2011. He was signed from MLS club Chivas USA and played mainly in domestic and European Cup matches until 2012, while Brad Friedel played the Premier League games. In October 2009, Guzan saved three penalties in a shootout win against Sunderland in a league cup contest after saving one during the game as well. He helped the team reach the 2009-10 League Cup and 2014-15 FA Cup finals and left for Middlesbrough on a free transfer.

7. One of Villa's first star keepers was local lad Jimmy Warner, who played over 100 games between 1886 and 1892. He won the 1887 FA Cup by keeping a clean sheet against the favorites, West Bromwich Albion, in a 2-0 victory. Warner was also in goal when Villa made its first appearance ever in the Football League in its inaugural season, 1888. He helped the team reach the 1891-92 FA Cup final, but they were beaten 3-0 by West Brom, and Warner was transferred to Newton Heath in Manchester several weeks later.

8. Billy George played for Villa between October 1897 and July 1911, appearing in approximately 400 games. He was signed for £50 from the Royal Artillery army side and helped Villa win First Division titles in 1898-99, 1899-1900, and 1909-10 as well as the 1904-05 FA Cup. George played three times for England and was sold to neighboring Birmingham City in 1911 as a player/trainer. He also played first-class and county cricket for several teams.

9. As of February 2021, former English international David James held the record for most Premier League appearances for a keeper at 572. He played 67 of those league games with Villa between 1999 and 2001. James was signed from Liverpool for £1.8 million and posted a clean sheet in his Villa debut. He led the team to the 1999-2000 FA Cup final, but Villa was beaten 1-0 by Chelsea. James played 85 games for the club before being sold to West Ham United for £3.5 million in July 2001.

10. Another famous Premier League keeper, Peter Schmeichel, had a brief stint at Villa Park. The great Danish international was regarded as one of the world's best due to his performances with Manchester United and his national side. Schmeichel had won numerous team and individual trophies by the time he signed with Villa from Sporting Lisbon in 2001. He played just one season with the club, though, appearing in 36 games. In October 2001, he became the first keeper to score a Premier League goal, in a 3-2 loss at Everton.

CHAPTER 5:

DARING DEFENDERS

QUIZ TIME!

1. Which defender holds the record for most appearances in all competitions for Villa as of 2020?

   a. Thomas Mort

   b. Tommy Smart

   c. Allan Evans

   d. Charlie Aitken

2. Allan Evans scored over 70 goals in all competitions for Villa.

   a. True

   b. False

3. Who scored four goals in the 1992-93 Premier League season?

   a. Steve Staunton

   b. Paul McGrath

   c. Earl Barret

   d. Neil Cox

4. Who was the only defender to be shown a red card in the 2007-08 Premier League season?

    a. Zat Knight
    b. Martin Laursen
    c. Wilfred Bouma
    d. Curtis Davies

5. How many goals did Ciaran Clark tally in all competitions in 2010-11?

    a. 11
    b. 7
    c. 4
    d. 1

6. Who played 3,439 minutes in the 1994-95 Premier League season?

    a. Phil King
    b. Shaun Teale
    c. Steve Staunton
    d. Ugo Ehiogu

7. James Chester was the only defender to score a goal for the team in 2016-17.

    a. True
    b. False

8. Which player earned five assists in the 2017-18 English Championship Division season?

    a. Alan Hutton
    b. John Terry

c. Ahmed Elmohamady

d. James Chester

9. Which season did Paul McGrath win the PFA Players' Player of the Year award?

   a. 1995-96

   b. 1994-95

   c. 1992-93

   d. 1989-90

10. Which defender played 2,903 minutes in the 2019-20 Premier League season?

    a. Frédéric Guilbert

    b. Ezri Konsa

    c. Matt Targett

    d. Tyrone Mings

11. Who was shown five yellow cards in all competitions in 2003-04?

    a. Olof Mellberg

    b. Ronny Johnsen

    c. Mark Delaney

    d. Ulises de la Cruz

12. Martin Laursen made 91 appearances in all competitions for Villa.

    a. True

    b. False

13. How many defenders scored at least two goals in all competitions in 2015-16?

a. 5

b. 3

c. 1

d. 0

14. How many goals did Martin Laursen score in his Villa career?

   a. 5

   b. 8

   c. 11

   d. 15

15. Who made 45 appearances in all competitions in 2008-09?

   a. Carlos Cuéllar

   b. Luke Young

   c. Curtis Davies

   d. Nicky Shorey

16. Charlie Aitken made over 650 appearances in all competitions for Villa.

   a. True

   b. False

17. Which defender was shown seven yellow cards in the 1992-93 Premier League season?

   a. Shaun Teale

   b. Dean Saunders

   c. Bryan Small

   d. Neil Cox

18. Who played all 38 matches in the 2002-03 Premier League campaign?

    a. Ronny Johnsen
    b. Olof Mellberg
    c. Ulises de la Cruz
    d. Rob Edwards

19. How many goals did Steve Staunton score in all competitions with Villa?

    a. 8
    b. 10
    c. 16
    d. 20

20. Fans dubbed defender Olof Mellberg's final home game with Aston Villa "Mellberg Day."

    a. True
    b. False

QUIZ ANSWERS

1. D – Charlie Aitken

2. B – False

3. B – Paul McGrath

4. A – Zat Knight

5. C – 4

6. D – Ugo Ehiogu

7. B – False

8. C – Ahmed Elmohamady

9. C – 1992-93

10. D – Tyrone Mings

11. C – Mark Delaney

12. A – True

13. B – 3

14. C – 11

15. C – Curtis Davies

16. A – True

17. A – Shaun Teale

18. B – Olof Mellberg

19. D – 20

20. A – True

DID YOU KNOW?

1. With 660 games under his belt, defender Charlie Aitken is currently number one for all-time career appearances with Villa. The native of Scotland played from August 1959 to May 1976 after showing up at the club with friend Wilson Briggs to try out for the team. Both players were given contracts, but Briggs played just twice with the first-team, while Aitken lasted 17 years. Aitken won the league cup in 1974-75 after losing in the 1962-63 and 1970-71 finals and won the Third Division title in 1970-71. After leaving Villa, he joined the New York Cosmos in America.

2. Howard Spencer made 294 appearances between 1894 and 1907 and was known as the "Prince of Full-Backs" for his solid play and sportsmanship. He originally joined the team in 1892 after playing for several amateur sides and made his pro debut in October 1894 when he was 18 years old. Spencer helped Villa win three First Division titles and three FA Cups and played six times for England.

3. Republic of Ireland international Paul McGrath cost £400,000 from Manchester United in August 1989 and became an instant success due to his fine defending and commitment. He helped the team finish as First Division runner-up in his first campaign, and two years later, he was named PFA Player of the Year. He then helped Villa place as runner-up in the inaugural Premier League campaign

and won two league cups with the side. McGrath played 322 times before joining Derby County in 1996.

4. Former Villa skipper Allan Evans of Scotland started his career as a striker but excelled as a central defender after making the switch. He arrived from Dunfermline Athletic in 1977 and remained until leaving for Leicester City in 1989. While at Villa Park, Evans helped the side win a First Division title as well as the European Cup and European Super Cup. Known for his determination and aggression, he played 475 games and chipped in with over 60 goals.

5. Rugged defender Shaun Teale of England joined from Bournemouth in 1991 and played 181 games before leaving for the Tranmere Rovers in 1995. The former decorator and painter provided Villa with the defensive stability the club was looking for, and Teale played his role very well alongside Paul McGrath. He helped the team finish the inaugural Premier League season as runner-up to Manchester United as well as beating United 3-1 in the 1993-94 League Cup final.

6. Unfortunately for Wilfred Bouma, he played just 90 times for Villa between 2005 and 2010 due to a series of injuries. The Dutch international arrived from PSV Eindhoven in August 2005 and soon became a cult hero because of his tackling skills and approach to the game. He scored just one goal for Villa and made only two appearances in his final two seasons, both in 2008-09. Bouma returned to PSV in June 2010 and stayed healthy enough to play just over 100 games before retiring three years later.

7. Another defender who made a big impact in a short time at Villa was England's Earl Barrett. He joined from Oldham Athletic in February 1992 in the final season of the First Division. The athletic and classy right-back was well worth his £1.7 million transfer fee, as he played in every game of the inaugural Premier League campaign when Villa finished as runner-up. He also helped the side down mighty Manchester United in 1993-94 to lift the league cup. Barrett played 150 games before leaving for Everton in January 1995.

8. Welsh international Mark Delaney played just under 200 times for Villa before being forced to retire in 2007 due to a serious knee injury at the age of 31. He arrived from Cardiff City in March 1999 and was a packer in a wool factory before turning to football. The steady defender helped the team reach the FA Cup final in 1999-2000, but he began to have problems with his knee the following season. After hanging up his boots, Delaney stayed with the club as a youth coach, became boss of the Under-23 squad, and was still with the club in 2021.

9. At just 5 feet 4 inches tall, Alan Wright of England beat the odds by enjoying an exceptional career and playing 329 times for Villa. He played in two Wembley Cup finals as he won the 1995-96 League Cup and took home a runner-up medal from the 1999-2000 FA Cup. Wright signed from Blackburn Rovers in 1995 for £900,000. He chipped in with five goals before leaving for Middlesbrough in 2003.

10. English international Tommy Smart made over 450 appearances for the club between 1920 and 1934, after arriving from nearby Halesowen Town. He played five times for England and also represented the Football League XI. Smart played Army soccer during World War I before resuming his career and was a member of the 1924 side that played Scotland in England's first-ever match at Wembley Stadium. He helped Villa win the 1919-20 FA Cup and reach the 1923-24 final. Just six players have appeared in more games for Villa than Smart.

CHAPTER 6:

MAESTROS OF THE MIDFIELD

QUIZ TIME!

1. Which midfielder made the most career appearances for Villa?

   a. Dennis Mortimer

   b. Gordon Cowans

   c. Vic Crowe

   d. Gareth Barry

2. David Platt won the PFA Players' Player of the Year award in 1989-90.

   a. True

   b. False

3. Who tallied nine goals in the 1992-93 Premier League season?

   a. David Farrell

   b. Kevin Richardson

   c. Ray Houghton

   d. Garry Parker

4. How many goals did Conor Hourihane net in the 2018-19 domestic league?

    a. 4
    b. 7
    c. 9
    d. 12

5. Which midfielder played 3,261 minutes in all competitions in 2013-14?

    a. Leandro Bacuna
    b. Marc Albrighton
    c. Ashley Westwood
    d. Yacouba Sylla

6. Who scored five goals in the 2004-05 Premier League?

    a. Gavin McCann
    b. Steven Davis
    c. Thomas Hitzlsperger
    d. Lee Hendrie

7. Glenn Whelan earned five assists in the 2018-19 English Championship Division season.

    a. True
    b. False

8. Which midfielder was the only Villa player to be shown a red card in the 1994-95 Premier League campaign?

    a. Kevin Richardson
    b. Ray Houghton
    c. Ian Taylor

d. Andy Townsend

9. How many assists did James Milner post in the 2009-10 Premier League?

    a. 2
    b. 5
    c. 8
    d. 12

10. Which midfielder registered five goals in the 2013-14 Premier League?

    a. Leandro Bacuna
    b. Fabian Delph
    c. Karim El Ahmadi
    d. Yacouba Sylla

11. Who appeared in 40 matches in all competitions in 2008-09?

    a. Ashley Young
    b. Stiliyan Petrov
    c. Gareth Barry
    d. Craig Gardner

12. Gordon Cowans had three separate playing stints with Villa.

    a. True
    b. False

13. How many appearances did Dennis Mortimer make in all competitions for the club?

a. 194

b. 262

c. 379

d. 403

14. Who scored four goals in the 2011-12 Premier League?

   a. Marc Albrighton

   b. Stiliyan Petrov

   c. Barry Bannan

   d. Chris Herd

15. How many goals did Ashley Young contribute in the 2007-08 Premier League season?

   a. 16

   b. 14

   c. 8

   d. 5

16. Fan favorite Ian Taylor became a club ambassador after hanging up his boots.

   a. True

   b. False

17. Who scored 10 goals in all competitions in 1997-98?

   a. Lee Hendrie

   b. Ian Taylor

   c. Saša Ćurčić

   d. Scott Murray

18. Which former Villa midfielder holds the record for all-time games played in the Premier League?

a. George Boateng
b. Steve Stone
c. Paul Merson
d. Gareth Barry

19. How many goals did Gordon Cowans score in all competitions with Aston Villa?

    a. 26
    b. 43
    c. 59
    d. 66

20. Paul Merson joined Villa from Arsenal in 1998.

    a. True
    b. False

QUIZ ANSWERS

1. B – Gordon Cowans

2. A – True

3. D – Garry Parker

4. B – 7

5. C – Ashley Westwood

6. D – Lee Hendrie

7. B – False

8. D – Andy Townsend

9. D – 12

10. A – Leandro Bacuna

11. C – Gareth Barry

12. A – True

13. D – 403

14. B – Stiliyan Petrov

15. C – 8

16. A – True

17. B – Ian Taylor

18. D – Gareth Barry

19. C – 59

20. B – False

DID YOU KNOW?

1. Former Villa skipper Dennis Mortimer scored 36 goals in 403 matches between 1975 and 1985 and helped the club capture the First Division championship in 1980-81. There was more to come, too, as he led his teammates to the historic European Cup win in Rotterdam a year later. Mortimer was known for his consistent high-quality performances, but he never played nationally for England's senior squad. He also won a league cup and European Super Cup with Villa before joining Brighton and Hove Albion.

2. Gordon Cowans played for nine pro clubs during his career and enjoyed three stints with Villa. The English international was an apprentice in 1974 and turned pro in 1976. He helped the side win a league cup, First Division title, European Cup, and the European Super Cup before leaving in 1985, and he was named PFA Young Player of the Year for 1980-81. He returned to Villa from 1988 to 1991 and again in 1993-94. Cowans played over 500 games. He contributed 59 goals for Villa and later returned in a coaching role and became an assistant manager.

3. One of Villa's most vital midfielders between December 1994 and 2003 was local player and fan favorite Ian Taylor. He arrived in mid-season from Sheffield Wednesday, scored in his debut, and helped the team win the 1995-96

League Cup. The former forklift driver was a lifelong Villa supporter who made 290 appearances and contributed over 40 goals. He became a club ambassador after hanging up his boots and also worked as a media pundit. Taylor displayed a tremendous passion for the club but was released in 2003 and joined Derby County, where he was made team captain and led the side in scoring in his first season there.

4. Former captain and English international Paul Merson may have had his troubles off the pitch, but he was a spark plug on it for Villa. Merson displayed magical ball control after signing in 1998 for £6.75 million from Middlesbrough. He scored in his debut and helped the side reach the 1999-2000 FA Cup final and win its Intertoto Cup stage in 2001. Merson's on-pitch flair resulted in winning the Players' and Supporters' Player of the Year awards in 2000. He left for Portsmouth on a free transfer in 2002 after 144 appearances and 19 goals with Villa.

5. Born in Birmingham, Mark Walters kicked off his pro career with Villa from 1981 to 1987 and racked up 48 goals in just over 220 contests before joining Glasgow Rangers. He won the FA Youth Cup with the club in 1980 and signed as a professional a year later. He wasn't on the squad that won the 1981-82 European Cup, but he did win the 1982 European Super Cup with the side in January 1983. Walters also helped Villa earn promotion back to the top flight by finishing as Second Division runner-up in 1987-88 after being relegated the previous season.

6. Regarded as one of the greatest players of his era, Northern Ireland international Robert Dennis "Danny" Blanchflower was skipper of the Villa teams he played for between 1951 and 1954. The defensive midfielder was known for his leadership, passing accuracy, and tempo. He joined from Barnsley and was sold to Tottenham Hotspur, where he won several individual and team awards. Blanchflower notched 10 goals in 155 Villa outings and later managed Northern Ireland and Chelsea. His brother Jackie played for Manchester United.

7. As of February 2021, former Villa skipper Gareth Barry held the record for most Premier League games played in history at 653 and also appeared 53 times for England. Barry moved to Villa from Brighton and Hove Albion as a youngster in 1997 and remained until leaving for Manchester City in 2009. He played 440 times, including 365 in the Premier League, and scored 52 goals before being sold for £12 million in June 2009. Barry helped the side advance to the UEFA Cup by winning their stage of the 2001 Intertoto Cup.

8. English-born Scottish international Bruce Rioch joined Villa from Luton Town in 1969 and left in 1974 when he transferred to Derby County. He cost Villa £100,000, which was then a record fee dished out by a Second Division club. Rioch helped the side reach the 1970-71 League Cup final, where they were beaten 2-0 by Tottenham Hotspur. He played 176 games as a dependable midfielder and contributed 37 goals before being sold for £200,000.

9. Vic Crowe was a fine Welsh international whose family moved to Birmingham when he was two years old. He spent his youth career with West Bromwich Albion but signed with Villa in 1951 and remained until 1964 when he left for Peterborough United. He played over 350 games and scored two goals with Villa. Crowe missed the 1956-57 FA Cup final because of injury but captained the team to the Second Division title in 1959-60 and the league cup in 1960-61. He also managed Villa from 1970 to 1974 and won the Division Three title in 1971-72.

10. English international Jack Grealish was appointed Villa captain in March 2019 even after being involved in several off-pitch episodes. He was born in Birmingham, and his great-grandfather was team legend Billy Garraty. Grealish joined the club as a youth and spent 2013-14 on loan with Notts County. He helped Villa win the Championship League playoffs in 2018-19 as well as reach the FA Cup final in 2014-15 and league cup final in 2019-20. He was named Aston Villa Player of the Season for 2019-20, the Young Player of the Season in 2014-15, and to the PFA Championship League Team of the Year for 2018-19. As of February 2021, Grealish had played just over 200 games for Villa with 32 goals to his name.

CHAPTER 7:

SENSATIONAL STRIKERS & FORWARDS

QUIZ TIME!

1. Which player has made the most appearances as a forward for Villa as of 2020?

   a. Gabriel Agbonlahor
   b. Johnny Dixon
   c. Billy Walker
   d. Joe Bache

2. Juan Pablo Ángel scored 14 goals in all competitions in 2004-05.

   a. True
   b. False

3. How many goals did Dalian Atkinson score in the 1992-93 Premier League?

   a. 11
   b. 8
   c. 5
   d. 3

4. Which player scored seven goals in the 2012-13 domestic league?

   a. Darren Bent
   b. Andreas Weimann
   c. Charles N'Zogbia
   d. Brett Holman

5. How many goals did Peter Withe score in all competitions for Villa?

   a. 61
   b. 77
   c. 85
   d. 90

6. What nickname was Dwight Yorke given by the Villa fans?

   a. Dwight the Knight
   b. The Man from Canaan
   c. Sir Dwight
   d. The Smiling Assassin

7. Dean Saunders played 43 matches in all competitions in 1994-95.

   a. True
   b. False

8. How many assists did Jack Grealish record in the 2019-20 Premier League?

   a. 3
   b. 4

c. 6

d. 10

9. Which player was shown seven yellow cards in the 2014-15 domestic league?

    a. Carles Gil

    b. Christian Benteke

    c. Andreas Weimann

    d. Gabriel Agbonlahor

10. Thomas Waring scored a hat-trick in his debut against which club?

    a. Birmingham City

    b. Leicester City

    c. Arsenal FC

    d. Sheffield United

11. How many goals did John Carew score in all competitions in 2008-09?

    a. 6

    b. 8

    c. 11

    d. 15

12. Gabriel Agbonlahor played his entire pro career with Aston Villa.

    a. True

    b. False

13. For which season did Andy Gray win the PFA Players' Player of the Year award with Villa?

a. 1986-87

b. 1984-85

c. 1976-77

d. 1975-76

14. Who scored nine goals in the 1999-2000 Premier League?

    a. Darius Vassell

    b. Richard Walker

    c. Julian Joachim

    d. Benny Carbone

15. Who made 40 appearances in all competitions in 1996-97?

    a. Dwight Yorke

    b. Savo Milošević

    c. Mark Draper

    d. Tommy Johnson

16. Winger Albert Adomah recorded 13 assists in the 2016-17 Championship League.

    a. True

    b. False

17. Who was the only player to be shown a red card in all competitions in 2018-19?

    a. Albert Adomah

    b. Andre Green

    c. Jack Grealish

    d. Anwar El Ghazi

18. Which player tallied four goals in the 2004-05 domestic league?

a. Juan Pablo Ángel

b. Patrik Berger

c. Kevin Phillips

d. Gabriel Agbonlahor

19. How many goals did Darius Vassell contribute in the 2003-04 Premier League?

    a. 12

    b. 9

    c. 7

    d. 4

20. Billy Walker made over 600 appearances for Villa.

    a. True

    b. False

QUIZ ANSWERS

1. C – Billy Walker

2. B – False

3. A – 11

4. B – Andreas Weimann

5. D – 90

6. D – The Smiling Assassin

7. A – True

8. C – 6

9. D – Gabriel Agbonlahor

10. A – Birmingham City

11. D – 15

12. A – True

13. C – 1976-77

14. C – Julian Joachim

15. A – Dwight Yorke

16. B – False

17. D – Anwar El Ghazi

18. C – Kevin Phillips

19. B – 9

20. B – False

DID YOU KNOW?

1. Brian Little joined Villa in 1969 as an apprentice and turned pro in 1971, scoring in his full debut. As a teenager, he helped the club win the FA Youth Cup and then helped the first-team hoist the league cup in 1974-75 and 1976-77, scoring twice in the 1977 final. He also won the Third Division title with the squad in 1971-72. Little tallied 82 goals in 301 games before retiring in 1980 at the age of 26 due to injury. He managed the side from 1994 to 1998 and won the 1995-96 League Cup before resigning.

2. Leonard "King" Capewell signed as a semi-professional in 1921 from Wellington Town and turned pro a year later. The English forward played with the club until 1930 and posted 100 goals in 157 contests. During World War I, Capewell served with the Royal Engineers in Belgium. After hitting the century mark in goals for Villa, he was transferred to Walsall in February 1930. Capewell scored 88 times in 144 league outings and added 12 goals in 13 FA Cup matches.

3. Dwight Yorke was discovered by Villa boss Graham Taylor during a pre-season tour of Trinidad and Tobago. Taylor offered the 17-year-old a trial with the team. Yorke passed the audition and went on to play over 280 games from 1990 to 1998 before leaving for Manchester United. He started as a winger and then moved to center-forward.

He notched close to 100 goals for the team, helping it win the 1995-96 League Cup.

4. Christian Benteke arrived at Villa Park from Genk in his homeland of Belgium in the summer of 2012 for a reported £7 million. He scored in his debut and led the team with 23 goals in all competitions in his first season. Benteke scored another 26 goals in 62 games over the next two seasons and took home an FA Cup runner-up medal in 2014-15. He was then sold to Liverpool when the Merseyside club paid his contract release clause of a reported £32.5 million.

5. Winger Tony Morley will forever be remembered by Villa fans for providing Peter Withe with the cross that led to the winning goal in the 1981-82 European Cup final. Morley was one of the team's quickest and most exciting players between 1979 and 1983 and also helped the squad capture the 1980-81 First Division and the 1982 European Super Cup. He posted 34 goals in 180 games before joining West Bromwich Albion. Morley will also be remembered for winning the 1980-81 Goal of the Season award for his strike against Everton.

6. Tammy Abraham spent his youth career with Chelsea and was loaned to Villa in 2018-19. Playing in the second-tier Championship League, Abraham became just one of a few Villa players to net over 20 goals in a league campaign when he scored 25 in 37 games. Four of those goals came in a 5-5 home draw with Nottingham Forest, and he became the first Villa player since Tom Waring in 1933 to

net goals in seven straight home matches. Abraham was named to the PFA Championship League Team of the Year and helped the team earn promotion to the Premier League by winning the league playoff final.

7. Before Tammy Abraham, the last Villa player to notch 25 goals in a league campaign was Scottish international Andy Gray. He banged in 29 in 1976-77 to share the top-flight Golden Boot and also won the league cup that season as well as the PFA Young Player and PFA Players' Player of the Year awards. Gray was 19 years old when he arrived in October 1975, but he left for the Wolverhampton Wanderers in September 1979 for a then English-record transfer fee of £1.49 million. He returned to Villa in July 1985 for £150,000 and was sold to West Bromwich Albion in September 1987. Gray notched 54 goals in 113 league games with Villa.

8. Aston Villa was the second stop in Tony Hateley's career, which saw him suit up with a dozen different clubs. The striker joined from Notts County in 1963 and played until heading to Chelsea in 1966. Hateley once netted four second-half goals to help Villa erase a 5-1 deficit and earn a 5-5 draw with Tottenham Hotspur. He scored 86 goals in 148 games before being sold for £100,000, which was then a club record for Chelsea. Tony was the father of Mark Hateley and grandfather of Tom Hateley, both pro soccer players.

9. Frank Broome played for Villa from 1934 to 1946 while playing seven times for England. He joined from

Berkhamsted Town and helped the side earn promotion to the top flight in 1937-38 when it won the Second Division. His career with Villa was interrupted by World War II, and he made several guest appearances with other clubs at this time. Broome joined Derby County in 1946 after posting 91 goals in 151 contests.

10. With 49 goals in 144 outings between 1992 and 1995, Welsh international Dean Saunders was quite useful in front of the opposition goal. He arrived from Liverpool for a then club-record fee of £2.5 million and scored six times in his first four league matches. Villa finished the season as runner-up in the inaugural Premier League campaign and won the 1993-94 League Cup, with Saunders tallying twice in the 3-1 win over Manchester United. He was named the Supporters' Player of the Year in 1994-95 but was sold to the Turkish club Galatasaray in July 1995 for £2.35 million.

CHAPTER 8:

NOTABLE TRANSFERS & SIGNINGS

QUIZ TIME!

1. Which player is Villa's most expensive signing as of 2020?

    a. Darren Brent

    b. Tyrone Mings

    c. Wesley Moraes

    d. Ollie Watkins

2. In 2011-12, Villa signed Robert Pires, who was 37 years old at the time.

    a. True

    b. False

3. From which Scottish club did Villa sign Andy Gray in 1975-76?

    a. Dundee United

    b. Celtic FC

    c. Kilmarnock FC

    d. Rangers FC

4. With what club did Dwight Yorke sign in 1998-99?

    a. Blackburn Rovers

    b. Manchester United

    c. Liverpool FC

    d. Sunderland AFC

5. What was the transfer fee Villa paid to sign Ollie Watkins?

    a. €20.75 million

    b. €26 million

    c. €30.8 million

    d. €34 million

6. Who did Villa sign from Coventry City FC for €8.6 million in 1998-99?

    a. Dion Dublin

    b. Alan Thompson

    c. Paul Merson

    d. Steve Stone

7. Aston Villa did not sign any players in the 1992-93 season; they only promoted from within.

    a. True

    b. False

8. From which club did Villa sign Ashley Young in 2006-07?

    a. Wycombe Wanderers FC

    b. Preston North End

    c. Sheffield Wednesday

    d. Watford FC

9. For how much did the club sell Ugo Ehiogu to Middlesbrough FC in 2000-01?

    a. €5 million
    b. €8.75 million
    c. €10 million
    d. €12.2 million

10. Who did Villa acquire from Newcastle United in 2008-09?

    a. Curtis Davies
    b. Steve Sidwell
    c. James Milner
    d. Carlos Cuéllar

11. Which player was sold for the club's highest received transfer fee?

    a. Stewart Downing
    b. Christian Benteke
    c. Dwight Yorke
    d. James Milner

12. Pierluigi Gollini was the only player Villa signed from a club outside of England in 2016-17.

    a. True
    b. False

13. Who was the only player who did NOT leave Villa on a free transfer in 2012-13?

    a. James Collins
    b. Stephen Warnock
    c. Mason Watkins
    d. Carlos Cuéllar

14. From which club did Villa sign Wesley Moraes in 2019-20?

   a. FC Porto
   b. Itabuna EC
   c. Club Brugge KV
   d. AS Trenčín

15. What issue did Gustavo Bartelt face after being signed by Villa in 2000-01?

   a. There was a communication mix-up, and he arrived at Birmingham City FC by mistake.
   b. He refused to leave his former club, AS Roma.
   c. The mandatory physical revealed he had three broken bones, and the signing fell through.
   d. He was arrested for having a fake passport.

16. Christian Benteke was sold to Liverpool FC for a record fee of €46.5 million.

   a. True
   b. False

17. How many players did Villa sign in 2017-18?

   a. 5
   b. 12
   c. 2
   d. 7

18. How much did Villa pay Fulham FC to acquire Ross McCormack in 2016-17?

   a. €20 million
   b. €17.25 million

c. €15 million

d. €14.3 million

19. How many matches did David Unsworth play for Villa before transferring to Everton FC in 1998-99?

    a. 1

    b. 3

    c. 5

    d. 8

20. In 2014-15, the club signed three players from Valencia FC.

    a. True

    b. False

QUIZ ANSWERS

1. D – Ollie Watkins

2. A – True

3. A – Dundee United

4. B – Manchester United

5. C – €30.8 million

6. A – Dion Dublin

7. B – False

8. D – Watford FC

9. D – €12.2 million

10. C – James Milner

11. B – Christian Benteke

12. A – True

13. A – James Collins

14. C – Club Brugge KV

15. D – He was arrested for having a fake passport.

16. A – True

17. C – 2

18. D – €14.3 million

19. B – 3

20. A – True

DID YOU KNOW?

1. As of February 2021, the highest reported transfer fees paid for players by Aston Villa are: forward Ollie Watkins from Brentford FC for €30.8 million in 2020-21; forward Wesley Moraes from Club Brugge KV for €25 million in 2019-20; defender Tyrone Mings from AFC Bournemouth for €22.3 million in 2019-20; forward Darren Bent from Sunderland AFC for €21.5 million in 2010-11; and forward Bertrand Traoré from Olympique Lyon for €18.4 million in 2020-21.

2. The highest reported fees received for transferred players by the club are: forward Christian Benteke to Liverpool FC for €46.5 million in 2015-16; midfielder Stewart Downing to Liverpool FC for €22.8 million in 2011-12; midfielder James Milner to Manchester City for €22.0 million in 2010-11; forward Dwight Yorke to Manchester United for €19.25 million in 1998-99; and midfielder Ashley Young to Manchester United for €18 million in 2011-12.

3. Forward Oliver "Ollie" Watkins began his career with Exeter City and won the EFL Young Player of the Year Award in 2016-17. He joined Brentford in 2017 and stayed until September 2020 when he signed with Villa for a club-record fee of €30.8 million. Watkins shared the second-tier English Championship Golden Boot in 2019-20 with 25 goals in 46 league games and was named the league's

player of the year. He got off to a flying start with Villa in 2020-21 by notching 12 goals in his first 23 matches, including a hat-trick in a 7-2 home victory over defending Premier League champions Liverpool.

4. Villa manager John Gregory didn't want to sell Dwight Yorke to Manchester United in 1998 unless United was prepared to include fellow striker Andy Cole as part of the transaction. However, Yorke asked and pushed for a transfer. He then played for Villa on opening day of the 1998-99 Premier League campaign at Everton but appeared disinterested and put in minimal effort. Since it appeared Yorke was prepared to sulk until he was moved, Gregory caved and sent him to Man United on August 20 for a reported €19.25 million.

5. Welsh international Trevor Ford was a physical center-forward who created plenty of space to score goals. He notched 23 in 38 games for his homeland and added 61 in 128 appearances with Villa, with 60 coming in 120 league outings. Ford joined the team from Swansea Town in January 1947 for £9,500 and left for Sunderland in October 1950 for a then-record transfer fee for a British player of £30,000. Ford led Villa in scoring for three straight seasons, from 1947-48 to 1949-50, and was also an avid cricket player.

6. When striker Peter Withe joined Villa from Newcastle United in 1980, he cost a club-record £500,000 at the time. It was money well spent, though, as he notched 20 goals in

his first season to help the team win the 1980-81 First Division title. He then scored the lone goal in the 1981-82 European Cup final and also helped win the 1982 European Super Cup. Withe notched 90 goals in 232 games before leaving for Sheffield United. He later returned to Villa as a scout and assistant manager.

7. Former Villa captain Gareth Southgate was a classy and reliable central defender who arrived from Crystal Palace for £2.5 million in July 1995. Southgate was then converted from a midfielder to a center-back. He helped the side win the league cup in his first season while also qualifying for the UEFA Cup. He played every league game in 1998-99, and in the following campaign, he led the team to the FA Cup final, which they lost 1-0 to Chelsea. Southgate was sold to Middlesbrough for £6.5 million in July 2001 for a healthy profit.

8. Republic of Ireland international Steve Staunton enjoyed two spells with Villa and appeared in 350 matches. He was signed in 1991 from Liverpool for £1.1 million and headed back to the Merseyside club seven years later on a free transfer. But just two years after that, Staunton returned to Villa Park for three more years on a free transfer before heading to Coventry City. He provided steadiness as a defender and midfielder and helped Villa win the 1993-94 and 1995-96 League Cups. Staunton played 102 times for Ireland and later managed the team.

9. After arriving from Crewe Alexandra for £200,000, David Platt became a driving force in the Villa midfield from

1988 to 1991 until departing for Bari in Italy. He had a knack for scoring goals, as he tallied 62 of them in 139 outings. The English international helped Villa earn promotion to the top flight after his first season as Second Division runner-up, and they finished as runners-up again in 1989-90 to Liverpool in the First Division. Platt was voted the PFA Players' Player of the Year for 1989-90 and was named to the PFA First Division Team of the Year. He was then sold for a reported £6.5 million.

10. Colombian international forward Juan Pablo Ángel arrived in January 2001 for what was then a club-record £9.5 million from River Plate in Argentina. After a slow start because of injuries, illness in his family, and difficulty adapting to life in England, Ángel finally scored his first Villa goal in the 2000-01 Premier League finale. He then used his strength, aerial ability, and pace to lead the team in goals in 2003-04 with 23 in all competitions and 16 in the league. Ángel, who became a fan favorite, notched 62 goals in just over 200 games and left for the New York Red Bulls in 2007.

CHAPTER 9:

ODDS & ENDS

QUIZ TIME!

1. How many matches did Villa win in their first Premier League season?

   a. 14

   b. 17

   c. 21

   d. 24

2. Archie Hunter scored a goal in every round of the 1887 FA Cup.

   a. True

   b. False

3. In 1892, Villa set a club record by defeating which team 12-2?

   a. Tottenham Hotspur

   b. Chelsea FC

   c. Wednesbury Old Athletic

   d. Accrington FC

4. Villa's longest winning streak in domestic league competition lasted how many games?

    a. 17
    b. 14
    c. 10
    d. 8

5. Who was the youngest player to make an appearance for Villa's first team at 15 years and 148 days old?

    a. Chris Price
    b. Rushian Hepburn-Murphy
    c. Mick Wright
    d. Sil Swinkels

6. How many matches did the side win in the inaugural Football League season?

    a. 5
    b. 7
    c. 12
    d. 15

7. As of 2020, 77 players in Aston Villa's history have been capped by England's national team.

    a. True
    b. False

8. How many matches did the team lose in the 2015-16 Premier League?

    a. 27
    b. 30

c. 24

d. 32

9. What is the most goals Villa has scored in a Premier League campaign as of 2020?

   a. 71

   b. 65

   c. 57

   d. 48

10. Which player infamously scored all four goals in a 2-2 draw against Leicester City in 1976?

    a. Dennis Mortimer

    b. James Cumbes

    c. Chris Nicholl

    d. John Burridge

11. How many goals did the squad tally in 1930-31 to set the record for most top-flight goals in a Football League season?

    a. 134

    b. 128

    c. 117

    d. 109

12. Villa won just three matches in the 2015-16 Premier League.

    a. True

    b. False

13. Who is Villa's most-capped player for the English national team as of 2020?

    a. Alan Wright
    b. Gareth Southgate
    c. David Platt
    d. Ashley Young

14. What is the most wins Villa has recorded in a single domestic league season?

    a. 24
    b. 26
    c. 29
    d. 32

15. Aston Villa's first European match was against this club in the 1975-76 UEFA Cup.

    a. Real Sociedad
    b. AIK Fotboll
    c. Royal Antwerp FC
    d. Hertha Berlin

16. In 1898-99, Villa went on a 15-game streak without losing a match.

    a. True
    b. False

17. Villa's biggest victory in the Premier League era was against which club in 1994-95?

    a. Blackburn Rovers
    b. Wimbledon FC

c. Sheffield United

d. Ipswich Town

18. Who was the oldest player to make an appearance for Villa at the age of 40?

   a. Pepe Reina

   b. Robert Pires

   c. Brad Friedel

   d. Shay Given

19. What is the most points Villa has recorded in a season in any domestic league?

   a. 65

   b. 72

   c. 77

   d. 83

20. The most goals Villa has conceded in a domestic league season is 99 as of 2020.

   a. True

   b. False

QUIZ ANSWERS

1. C – 21
2. A – True
3. D – Accrington FC
4. C – 10
5. A – Chris Price
6. C – 12
7. B – False
8. A – 27
9. A – 71
10. C – Chris Nicholl
11. B – 128
12. A – True
13. B – Gareth Southgate
14. D – 32
15. C – Royal Antwerp FC
16. B – False
17. B – Wimbledon FC
18. C – Brad Friedel
19. D – 83
20. B – False

DID YOU KNOW?

1. Aston Villa was one of the original founding members of the English Football League way back in 1888 and was also a founding member of the English Premier League in 1992. Villa is one of just five English soccer clubs to have won the European Cup/European Champions League.

2. Club co-founder Jack Hughes requested that the Aston Villa Football Club should consist of 15 players, with most of them coming from the Aston Villa Wesleyan Chapel cricket team. The soccer club was created to keep the cricket players active throughout the winter.

3. The club's first official home ground was Wellington Road in 1876. Team captain George Ramsay believed the team needed to play in an enclosed venue to collect an admission fee from supporters. Wellington Road was initially rented by the club on a three-year lease.

4. Villa has a fierce rivalry with fellow Birmingham-based club Birmingham City. The first competition between the clubs took place in 1879. This fixture is commonly known as the Second City Derby. The team also has a heated rivalry with fellow Midlands club West Bromwich Albion and has less intense rivalries with nearby Wolverhampton Wanderers and Coventry City.

5. The traditional kit colors consist of claret shirts, sky blue sleeves, white shorts with claret and blue trim, and sky

blue socks with claret and white trim. The traditional club badge features a rampant lion. The claret color was originally a shade of chocolate brown that eventually became claret.

6. In the early years, the team's colors were typically plain white, gray, or blue shirts with either black or white shorts. Between 1877 and 1879, the squad wore several different kits which included white, black, blue, red, and green. In 1880, black jerseys were introduced with a red lion sewn into the chest, and these were worn for the next six years.

7. Soccer was an amateur sport in England until it turned professional in 1885, but with a national wage limit or salary cap across the board for each player. Villa director William McGregor believed low attendances at friendly matches were hurting the sport and proposed the country's top teams join together to form a league. This led to the formation of the English Football League in 1888.

8. The club in 2007 introduced a new badge that includes a star to represent the team's European Cup victory in 1981-82. The background behind the rampant lion is blue. and the team's motto of "Prepared" remained in the badge. However, the Aston Villa name was shortened to AVFC. The badge was changed again in 2016 with claws being added to the lion and the "Prepared" motto being removed.

9. Villa Park is the eighth-largest soccer stadium in England and the largest in the Midlands area. It became the first

English venue to host international games in three different centuries, and it has hosted a record 55 FA Cup semifinal matches. The club's training facilities are situated at Bodymoor Heath in north Warwickshire.

10. Aston Villa also has a women's soccer team that plays in the Women's Super League after being promoted in 2019-20 as champions of the second-tier FA Women's Championship. The side was originally founded in 1973 as Solihull FC and was taken over by Aston Villa in 1989.

CHAPTER 10:

DOMESTIC COMPETITION

QUIZ TIME!

1. What was the first trophy that Villa won?

    a. FA Charity Shield

    b. Sheriff of London Charity Shield

    c. Football League First Division

    d. FA Cup

2. Villa was the first Football League club to win the domestic double.

    a. True

    b. False

3. How many times has Villa won the domestic double of the league title and FA Cup?

    a. 4

    b. 3

    c. 1

    d. 0

4. Which club did Villa defeat to win their first FA Cup in 1887?

   a. Wolverhampton Wanderers
   b. Rangers FC
   c. West Bromwich Albion
   d. Blackburn Rovers

5. How many times has the club won the Football League Cup as of 2020?

   a. 7
   b. 5
   c. 3
   d. 1

6. Which side did Villa face in the 1996 Football League Cup final?

   a. Leeds United
   b. Notts County
   c. Queens Park Rangers
   d. Arsenal FC

7. As of 2020, Villa has never won the Premier League title.

   a. True
   b. False

8. Aston Villa faced which club in the 2015 FA Cup final?

   a. AFC Bournemouth
   b. Leicester City
   c. Middlesbrough FC
   d. Arsenal FC

9. How many times has Villa won the FA Youth Cup as of 2020?

    a. 0

    b. 1

    c. 3

    d. 5

10. Aston Villa shared the 1981 FA Charity Shield honors with which team?

    a. Manchester United

    b. Tottenham Hotspur

    c. Chelsea FC

    d. Manchester City

11. In 2018-19, Villa defeated which side to win the EFL Championship League playoffs?

    a. Derby County

    b. West Bromwich Albion

    c. Sheffield United

    d. Norwich City

12. Villa defeated Brighton and Hove Albion in the 1910 FA Charity Shield.

    a. True

    b. False

13. How many times has the team won the FA Cup as of 2020?

    a. 3

    b. 5

    c. 7

    d. 11

14. What is the unusual fact about Villa's 1977 Football League Cup victory?

    a. Half of Villa's starters were sick and replaced by youth squad members.
    b. Everton FC forfeited the match due to poor pitch conditions.
    c. It took three matches to decide a winner.
    d. The match was postponed by a year due to a scheduling conflict.

15. Villa defeated which squad to win the 1901 Sheriff of London Charity Shield?

    a. Corinthian FC
    b. Sunderland AFC
    c. Watford FC
    d. Newcastle United

16. Villa was the runner-up for the Premier League title in 2000-01.

    a. True
    b. False

17. How many times has the club won a domestic league title in any Football League division?

    a. 10
    b. 7
    c. 5
    d. 2

18. Villa defeated which outfit for its first Football League Cup in 1961?

    a. Chelsea FC

    b. Wolverhampton Wanderers

    c. Tottenham Hotspur

    d. Rotherham United

19. Which club did Villa play in the 1972 FA Charity Shield?

    a. Manchester United

    b. Queens Park Rangers

    c. Manchester City

    d. Arsenal FC

20. As of 2020, Villa has not won the FA Cup in the Premier League era.

    a. True

    b. False

QUIZ ANSWERS

1. D – FA Cup

2. B – False

3. C – 1

4. C – West Bromwich Albion

5. B – 5

6. A – Leeds United

7. A – True

8. D – Arsenal FC

9. C – 3

10. B – Tottenham Hotspur

11. A – Derby County

12. B – False

13. C – 7

14. C – It took three matches to decide a winner.

15. A – Corinthian FC

16. B – False

17. A – 10

18. D – Rotherham United

19. C – Manchester City

20. A – True

DID YOU KNOW?

1. As of 2020, Aston Villa had won seven top-flight English League championships as well as two in the second tier and one in the third tier. The club had also captured five League Cup titles, one FA Charity/Community Shield, and two Sheriff of London Charity Shield honors. The team was relegated six times, from the Premier League to the Championship League in 2015-16 and from Division 1 to Division 2 in 1935-36, 1958-59, 1966-67, and 1986-87. Villa was also relegated from Division 2 to Division 3 in 1969-70.

2. When Villa was relegated in 2015-16, it was the first time the club had played outside of the English Premier League since its inception in 1992-93. However, the side earned promotion back to the top flight in 2018-19.

3. Villa captured the First Division title in 1893-94, 1895-96, 1896-97, 1898-99, 1899-1900, 1909-10, and 1980-81. The team captured the Second Division title in 1937-38 and 1959-60 and was the playoff winner in 2018-19. Villa also won the Third Division championship in 1971-72.

4. The seven FA Cup championships won by the club came in 1886-87, 1894-95, 1896-97, 1904-05, 1912-13, 1919-20, and 1956-57. The English Football League Cup was hoisted in 1960-61, 1974-75, 1976-77, 1993-94, and 1995-96. The team won the FA Charity Shield/FA Community Shield in 1981

and lifted the Sheriff of London Charity Shield in 1899 and 1901.

5. The club's very first Football League match took place on September 8, 1888, a 1-1 stalemate with local rivals Wolverhampton Wanderers. The club's first league goal was credited to Tom Green. Villa finished the inaugural league campaign in second place behind Preston North End.

6. When the 2019-20 season concluded, Villa had spent 106 seasons in English soccer's top-tier division. This was second most in the country behind Everton FC, who held the record at 117 seasons. Aston Villa versus Everton has been the most often played fixture in the English top tier throughout history.

7. Villa currently holds the record for the most goals in a season by a top-flight team in England, as they tallied 128 times in the 1930-31 First Division campaign. This was one more than Arsenal, which won the league for the first time that season, with Villa placing second.

8. In the 1899-1900 campaign, Aston Villa's Billy Garraty was recognized as the top scorer in world soccer. He notched 27 goals in 33 league games and tallied a total of 30 goals in 39 outings in all competitions.

9. Aston Villa forward Archie Hunter was the first player to notch a goal in every round of the FA Cup when he achieved the feat in the 1887 campaign. In addition, the club's longest home undefeated streak in the FA Cup

lasted for 13 years, as they went 19 games without tasting defeat between 1888 and 1901.

10. As of February 2021, the following were the club's Premier League records: Most appearances, Gareth Barry (365); most goals, Gabriel Agbonlahor (73); the club's first Premier League goal, Dalian Atkinson; biggest win, 7-1 versus Wimbledon in 1995; and the fastest goal, Dwight Yorke (13 seconds). The following were club records in all competitions: Most appearances, Charlie Aitken (660); most goals, Billy Walker (244); and most goals in a season, Thomas "Pongo" Waring (50).

CHAPTER 11:

EUROPE & BEYOND

QUIZ TIME!

1. How many European Cup/Champions League titles has Villa won as of 2020?

    a. 1

    b. 2

    c. 3

    d. 5

2. The 1975-76 UEFA Cup was the first international tournament Villa competed in.

    a. True

    b. False

3. Which club eliminated Villa in the 1997-98 UEFA Europa League quarterfinals?

    a. S.S. Lazio

    b. Inter Milan

    c. FC Spartak Moscow

    d. Atlético Madrid

4. Who scored the winning goal for Villa in the second leg of the 1982-83 European Super Cup?

    a. Ken McNaught
    b. Gary Shaw
    c. Peter Withe
    d. Gordon Cowans

5. Which was the only year Aston Villa competed for the Intercontinental Cup?

    a. 1961
    b. 1979
    c. 1982
    d. 1993

6. Which club did Villa defeat in the 1982 European Cup final?

    a. Bayern Munich
    b. Juventus
    c. Hamburger SV
    d. Real Madrid

7. As of 2020, Villa has competed in the European Champions League six times.

    a. True
    b. False

8. Villa did NOT play against which of these clubs on its way to the 2001 Intertoto Cup final?

    a. Stade Rennais
    b. TSV 1860 München

c. FC Basel

d. NK Slaven Belupo

9. Who knocked Villa out in the 2000 Intertoto Cup semifinals?

    a. VfB Stuttgart

    b. Bradford City

    c. Celta Vigo

    d. Udinese Calcio

10. Which club did Villa defeat in the 1982-83 European Super Cup?

    a. FC Barcelona

    b. Liverpool FC

    c. Real Madrid

    d. Juventus

11. How many times has the club qualified to participate in the UEFA Cup as of 2020?

    a. 3

    b. 6

    c. 10

    d. 13

12. The club reached the semifinals of the 2001-02 UEFA Champions League.

    a. True

    b. False

13. Who scored the winning goal in the 1982 European Cup final?

a. Mark Walters

b. Andy Blair

c. Gary Shaw

d. Peter Withe

14. How many times did Villa win its Intertoto Cup stage to advance to the UEFA Cup?

    a. 5

    b. 4

    c. 2

    d. 1

15. Villa faced which team in an Intercontinental Cup final?

    a. Feyenoord

    b. CA Peñarol

    c. AC Milan

    d. Paris Saint-Germain

16. Villa is one of only five British clubs to win the European Cup/Champions League as of 2020.

    a. True

    b. False

17. Villa did NOT play against which club on its way to the 1982 European Cup final?

    a. RSC Anderlecht

    b. Valur

    c. CSKA Sofia

    d. Dynamo Berlin

18. Which was the only side Villa faced in the 2008 Intertoto Cup?

    a. Rhyl FC
    b. Grasshopper Zürich
    c. FK Riga
    d. Odense Boldklub

19. Which club eliminated Villa in the 1982-83 European Cup quarterfinals?

    a. Sporting CP
    b. Juventus
    c. AS Monaco
    d. Ajax

20. As of 2020, the furthest Aston Villa has ever advanced in the UEFA Europa League is the quarterfinals.

    a. True
    b. False

QUIZ ANSWERS

1. A – 1

2. A – True

3. D – Atlético Madrid

4. D – Gordon Cowans

5. C – 1982

6. A – Bayern Munich

7. B – False

8. B – TSV 1860 München

9. C – Celta Vigo

10. A – FC Barcelona

11. D – 13

12. B – False

13. D – Peter Withe

14. C – 2

15. B – CA Peñarol

16. A – True

17. C – CSKA Sofia

18. D – Odense Boldklub

19. B – Juventus

20. A – True

DID YOU KNOW?

1. Aston Villa is one of five English clubs to have won the European Cup/European Champions League. It won on May 26, 1982, in Rotterdam, Holland, by edging Bayern Munich 1-0 courtesy of a goal by forward Peter Withe in the 67th minute in front of 46,000 fans.

2. Several Villa players placed in the top scorers' list in the 1981-82 European Cup tournament. Dieter Hoeneß of Bayern Munich led the way with eight goals, while Villa's Tony Morley netted four goals. Both Gary Shaw and Peter Withe also made the list as they each chipped in with three.

3. Villa reached the 1981-82 European Cup final by beating Knattspyrnufélagið Valur of Iceland 7-0 on aggregate in the first round with a 5-0 home victory in the first leg followed by a 2-0 win away in the second leg. They edged German side BFC Dynamo 2-1 away in the first leg of the second round and advanced on the away-goals rule as they were blanked 1-0 at home in the second leg.

4. Once the 1981-82 European Cup knockout stage kicked off, Aston Villa drew 0-0 with Ukrainian club Dynamo Kyiv in the first leg of the quarterfinals and won the second leg 2-0 at home. They faced Anderlecht of Belgium in the semifinal and advanced to the final showdown after winning 1-0 at home in the first leg and drawing 0-0 away in the second leg.

5. By winning the European Cup in 1982, Aston Villa qualified for the 1982 UEFA (European) Super Cup against Spanish La Liga giant Barcelona, which had won the UEFA Cup Winners' Cup. Barcelona took the first leg 1-0 at Camp Nou on January 13, 1983, with Villa winning the second leg 3-0 at Villa Park on January 26.

6. Former player Tony Barton was Villa's manager for the team's European Cup and UEFA Super Cup triumphs. He was an assistant to manager Ron Saunders in 1980 when the side won its first top-flight league title for 71 years in 1980-81. Barton then took over as manager in February 1982 when Saunders resigned. Barton enjoyed tremendous success in Europe but was fired in May 1984.

7. Although Villa's 3-0 scoreline in the second leg of the 1982 UEFA Super Cup appeared to be quite decisive, the game was actually closer than it looks. The teams were level 1-1 on aggregate after 90 minutes, thanks to a Gary Shaw goal with 10 minutes remaining. This led to 30 minutes of extra time to settle a winner. Gordon Cowan put Villa ahead 2-1 10 minutes into extra time, and Ken McNaught added an insurance marker just four minutes later for a 3-1 victory on aggregate.

8. Villa has also achieved success in one other European competition as the side was a co-winner of the 2001 and 2008 UEFA Intertoto Cups. Originally known as the International Football Cup, this event was founded in 1961 and was a summer tournament for European clubs that

didn't qualify for one of the major UEFA events, such as the Champions League, UEFA Cup, or Cup Winners' Cup. The competition was abandoned after 2008 but not before Villa shared the somewhat complicated 2001 and 2008 titles.

9. With the club winning its 2001 Intertoto Cup stage, the Villa qualified for the first round of the UEFA Cup, bypassing the qualifying round. Villa took on NK Varteks of Croatia in the first match but was edged 3-2 at home after conceding the winner in the 85th minute. Villa won the second leg in Croatia when Mustapha Hadji scored just before the final whistle for a 1-0 victory, tying the fixture 3-3 on aggregate. However, NK Varteks advanced on the away-goals rule.

10. Legend has it that the Aston Villa reserve team enlisted in the British Army and was captured in June 1940 during the evacuation of Dunkirk. The players were held in an East German prisoner of war camp and were challenged to a game by a regiment of German guards. When the match was halted before full-time, the prisoners had a 27-0 lead, thanks mainly to the Villa reserve side.

CHAPTER 12:

TOP SCORERS

QUIZ TIME!

1. Which player was the club's first recorded top goal-scorer in the 1888-89 Football League?

   a. Archie Hunter

   b. Dennis Hodgetts

   c. Albert Allen

   d. John Devey

2. Dean Saunders led the side in scoring in the inaugural Premier League season with 13 goals.

   a. True

   b. False

3. Who holds the club record for most goals scored in all competitions as of 2020?

   a. Billy Walker

   b. Harry Hampton

   c. Joe Bache

   d. Thomas Waring

4. How many goals did Jordan Ayew score to lead the squad in the 2015-16 Premier League season?

   a. 25
   b. 14
   c. 11
   d. 7

5. Which two players led the team in scoring in the 2008-09 Premier League with 11 goals each?

   a. Gabriel Agbonlahor and Ashley Young
   b. James Milner and Emile Heskey
   c. Gabriel Agbonlahor and John Carew
   d. Steve Sidwell and James Milner

6. How many league goals did Billy Walker register for Villa?

   a. 196
   b. 214
   c. 222
   d. 241

7. Brian Godfrey was Villa's top goal-scorer in the 1969-70 domestic league with only six goals.

   a. True
   b. False

8. Who is Villa's current top all-time scorer in the Premier League?

   a. Gabriel Agbonlahor
   b. Dwight Yorke

    c. Gareth Barry

    d. Dion Dublin

9. Which player notched 29 goals to lead Villa in the 1960-61 domestic league?

    a. Peter McParland

    b. Gerry Hitchens

    c. Harry Burrows

    d. Tony Hateley

10. How many goals did Albert Allen net in 1888-89?

    a. 67

    b. 10

    c. 14

    d. 19

11. Which player led Villa with 17 markers in the 1996-97 Premier League?

    a. Andy Townsend

    b. Tommy Johnson

    c. Savo Milošević

    d. Dwight Yorke

12. Thomas Waring scored 50 goals in all competitions in 1930-31.

    a. True

    b. False

13. Who scored 170 career goals in all competitions for the team?

a. Peter McParland

b. Johnny Dixon

c. Eric Houghton

d. Dai Astley

14. How many goals did Tammy Abraham tally in the 2018-19 Championship League division?

    a. 16

    b. 21

    c. 25

    d. 30

15. Who scored Villa's first Premier League hat-trick?

    a. Dion Dublin

    b. Dwight Yorke

    c. Tommy Johnson

    d. Dean Saunders

16. As of 2020, three different Villa players have led the Premier League in scoring.

    a. True

    b. False

17. How many goals did Thomas Waring score in the 1930-31 domestic league?

    a. 26

    b. 38

    c. 42

    d. 49

18. Which player has never led Villa in scoring in a domestic league season?

    a. Juan Pablo Ángel
    b. Julian Joachim
    c. Christian Benteke
    d. Ashley Young

19. How many goals did Peter McParland score in 34 international matches for Northern Ireland?

    a. 10
    b. 7
    c. 13
    d. 4

20. Gabriel Agbonlahor scored 90 goals in all competitions for Villa.

    a. True
    b. False

QUIZ ANSWERS

1. C – Albert Allen
2. A – True
3. A – Billy Walker
4. D – 7
5. C – Gabriel Agbonlahor and John Carew
6. B – 214
7. B – False
8. A – Gabriel Agbonlahor
9. B – Gerry Hitchens
10. D – 19
11. D – Dwight Yorke
12. A – True
13. C – Eric Houghton
14. C – 25
15. D – Dean Saunders
16. B – False
17. D – 49
18. D – Ashley Young
19. A – 10
20. B – False

DID YOU KNOW?

1. Billy Walker's 244 goals in 531 appearances between 1919 and 1933 currently stands as the club's all-time scoring record. He tallied 214 league markers and 30 in FA Cup games while spending his entire career with Villa. Walker also chipped in with nine goals in 18 matches for England. He joined the team in 1914 as a youth and became a manager after retiring. He became the first player to score a hat-trick of penalty kicks in a Football League game when he achieved the feat in 1921 against Bradford City. Walker won the FA Cup in 1920 and is enshrined in the Aston Villa Hall of Fame.

2. English international Harry Hampton played between 1904 and 1920 and finished his career with the club just two goals behind Billy Walker with 242 in 372 games. He's also the team's all-time top league scorer with 215 goals to Walker's 214. He scored them in 338 games compared to 478 matches for Walker. Hampton won two FA Cups and a league title with the team and scored both goals in the 1905 FA Cup final against Newcastle United in a 2-0 victory. Walker also scored five times in a 10-0 thumping of Sheffield Wednesday in a 1912 league outing and shared the First Division scoring title in 1911-12 with 25 markers.

3. The club's top scorer in the Premier League era is Gabriel Agbonlahor. The former skipper notched 73 goals in 322

outings between 2005-06 and 2015-16. He chipped in with a total of 86 in all competitions until retiring at the age of 32 in March 2019. Agbonlahor also helped the side reach the 2009-10 League Cup and the 2014-15 FA Cup finals. He spent his entire pro career with Villa after being sent on loan briefly before making his league debut with the club in March 2006 as a 19-year-old.

4. In 1930-31, Thomas "Pongo" Waring set a club record by scoring 49 goals in the league and 50 times in all competitions. He joined Villa in 1928 from Tranmere Rovers, scoring a hat-trick in his debut for the reserve team, and he stayed with the side until leaving for Barnsley in 1935. The charismatic former captain tallied 167 times for Villa in 226 matches, with 159 of them coming in league action while posting 10 hat-tricks. Waring also registered two other seasons with at least 30 goals for the squad.

5. Ranking fourth on the current all-time Villa scoring parade is former English international forward Joe Bache, who played between 1900 and 1914. He helped the team capture two FA Cups and a league title and notched 184 goals in 474 outings. Bache acted as the club's reserve team coach in 1927-28, and his son David Bache became a famous car stylist who produced numerous designs, mainly for Rover.

6. Although former English international Eric Houghton was known for managing the club to the 1956-57 FA Cup and

being a Villa coach, director, and vice-president, he was also a high-scoring forward. Houghton spent 1927 to 1946 with the team as a player after signing as a 17-year-old, and he scored 170 goals in 392 non-wartime matches mainly due to his powerful shot. This resulted in five goals in seven appearances for England. Houghton was also a top-notch cricketer and is in the Aston Villa Hall of Fame.

7. Peter McParland is another Aston Villa Hall of Fame member who ranks as one of the club's top all-time scorers. The Northern Ireland international forward played with 10 pro clubs and enjoyed a stint with Villa between 1952 and 1962. He won the FA Cup in 1956-57 as well as the Second Division title in 1959-60 and the league cup in 1960-61. McParland, who was nicknamed "Packy," was the first English Football League player to score in and win both of the country's major domestic cups. He left for Wolverhampton with 121 goals to his name in 341 contests.

8. Shortly after World War II, forward Johnny Dixon joined Villa and went on to tally 144 goals in 430 official matches before retiring in 1961. He helped the team hoist the FA Cup in 1956-57, and, after hanging up his boots, he remained with the club. He played occasionally with the reserve teams after retiring and also coached the junior side for three years and became the reserve team's trainer. His best campaign was 1951-52 when he netted 28 goals.

9. Billy Garraty was an English forward who played just once for his national team but appeared in 259 games with

Villa and contributed 112 goals. He played between 1897 and 1908 and returned as a trainer in 1913. Garraty led the league with 27 goals in 1899-1900 when Villa retained the league title, and he also helped the squad win the 1904-05 FA Cup. Garraty's great-grandson is Jack Grealish, an England international and current Villa skipper as of February 2021.

10. Welsh international forward Dais Astley scored 12 goals in 13 outings for his national team and racked up 100 goals in 173 appearances with Villa. He joined the club from Charlton Athletic in 1931 and remained until 1936 when he was sold to Derby County. After hanging up his boots, he became a manager and took charge of clubs such as Inter Milan, Genoa, and Djurgårdens IF. Astley currently ranks 10th on the Villa all-time scoring list, sharing the spot with Len Capewell.

CONCLUSION

The book you've just enjoyed reading contains close to 150 years' worth of trivia, facts, records, information, and anecdotes about the famous Aston Villa soccer club since its formation in 1874.

We hope you've been entertained by the way we've retraced the team's history from day one to 2021. We've included the highs and lows, and we hope these moments have triggered some fine or not so fine memories for you. If you've been able to learn something new along the way, that's even better.

Villa may have fallen on lean times lately, but the team still provides its fans with plenty of thrills, action, and drama week after week.

We've tried to present the information in a lighthearted and fun manner when it comes to describing the players and managers. We realize there's still quite a bit of Villa history, and a lot of names that may be missing from these pages. And that's simply due to the century and a half of information and facts to deal with.

Many Villa supporters may know most of the answers to the quiz questions and likely have a few stories and facts of their own to share. With the knowledge you already possess and the information provided in the book, you should be in the perfect position to challenge fellow Villa supporters when it comes to quiz contests.

Aston Villa may not be the most successful or richest club in soccer or even in England, but that doesn't really matter to their loyal fans. Those who fill Villa Park week after week are there to cheer their team on and realize they could witness soccer history in the making on any given night.

Thanks for being a passionate Aston Villa supporter and taking the time to read through the club's latest trivia book.